THE SUN AND THE STARS

by Scarlett Jones
illustrated by Geoffrey McCormack

Harcourt
SCHOOL PUBLISHERS

Printed in China

ISBN 10: 0-15-351514-7
ISBN 13: 978-0-15-351514-9

Ordering Options
ISBN 10: 0-15-351213-X (Grade 3 Advanced Collection)
ISBN 13: 978-0-15-351213-1 (Grade 3 Advanced Collection)
ISBN 10: 0-15-358104-2 (package of 5)
ISBN 13: 978-0-15-358104-5 (package of 5)

2 3 4 5 6 7 8 9 10 985 12 11 10 09 08 07

High overhead, the sun shines down. You can feel it warm your face. Each day, heat and light from the sun travel millions of miles to reach the surface of the earth. Plants use the energy of the sun in order to grow. Animals rely on plants for food. Without the sun, life would not exist here on earth.

The sun resembles a large, yellow ball of fire that stays steady in the sky. It is the closest star to the earth. That is why it looks bigger and brighter than other stars.

The sun is the star at the center of our solar system. The earth and the other planets revolve around the sun.

The sun and the stars you see at night are similar in many ways. All stars consist of gases. One gas is called hydrogen. Hydrogen is used to make light and heat energy. It is light energy that we see coming from the stars at night. The heat energy from the sun warms the earth.

The rays of heat hit the earth, and the earth reflects some of the rays back into space. These rays heat up the air around the earth. Other rays go right into the earth's surface. They warm the ground and the oceans.

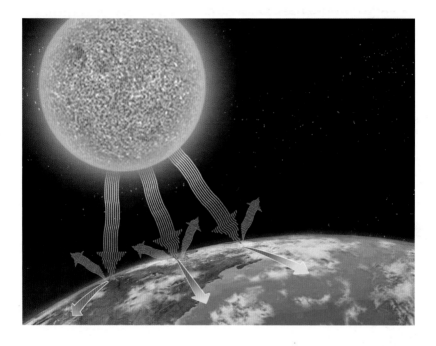

The sun is different from the earth in many ways. The earth is extremely small compared to the sun. In fact, the sun is so enormous that more than one million earths would fit inside it! The sun stays in one place in space. It does not move through space like the earth does. The sun rotates, or spins like a top.

The earth is made up mostly of rock and water, while the sun consists of very hot gases. The center, or core, of the sun is so hot that it would melt metal in an instant.

Scientists use special tools to study the sun because it is important to never look directly at the sun. Looking directly at the sun can harm your eyes.

Sometimes large flames, called solar flares, rise up from the surface of the sun. The picture on this page shows what a solar flare looks like.

Scientists have discovered large dark spots on the surface of the sun called sunspots. Sunspots are much cooler than other parts of the sun. Scientists watch the spots move to figure out how long it takes the sun to make one full rotation. Scientists have determined that it takes the sun approximately twenty-five to thirty-six days to make one complete rotation.

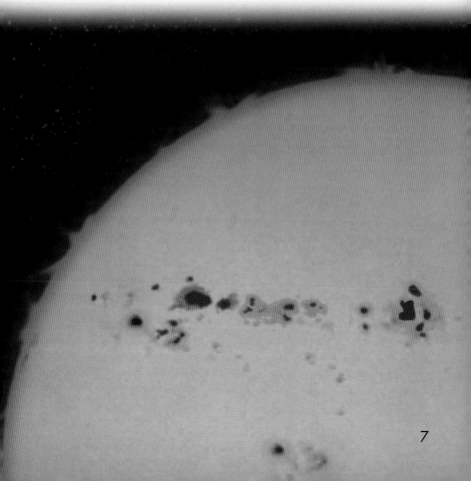

The sun and other stars are all made up of gases. However, stars differ in size. The sun is a medium-size star. The smallest star is called a red dwarf. It is difficult to see red dwarf stars in the sky because they are so small.

The sun is a yellow dwarf. Most yellow dwarf stars are larger than red dwarf stars. There are giant stars, too. A blue giant is an enormous star that is extremely hot. There are some giant stars that are approximately twenty times larger than the sun! The biggest stars of all are called super giant stars.

The color of a star tells us how hot it is. Think about how the flame of a campfire appears. The hottest part of a fire is closest to the wood, and this section of the flame is often blue. As the fire gets farther away from the wood, it gets cooler and becomes yellow. The coolest part of the fire is red. Just as in the colors of a campfire's flames, blue stars are the hottest, yellow stars are cooler, and red stars are the coolest.

The sun is approximately five billion years old. Some stars are older than the sun, and some stars are younger. Stars go through life cycles just like plants and animals do. Super giant stars are very old. As a super giant star burns up its gases, it becomes larger and larger. Eventually it explodes and shrinks to become a very small star called a white dwarf. White dwarf stars are among the oldest stars in space. Small- and medium-size stars, like our sun, will one day become white dwarf stars, too. Of course, this will not happen for another five billion years!

There are trillions of stars in space. Most stars are found in large groups called galaxies. One galaxy can have billions of stars in it. Galaxies are also made up of gases and dust, and they come in different sizes and shapes.

The earth and our sun are in a galaxy called the Milky Way. The Milky Way is shaped like a spiral with a large bulge in the middle. The sun is at one edge of one of the arms of the spiral. On a clear night, you can see the Milky Way in the sky. It looks like a milky strip of stars across the sky.

There are other spiral galaxies in space. The nearest galaxy to the Milky Way is called the Andromeda Galaxy. Scientists know that there are about thirty other spiral galaxies.

Another kind of galaxy has stars that are extremely close to one another. Since the stars are so close together these galaxies sometimes look like one huge star. The stars in these galaxies are very old. Some of these galaxies are long and stretched out like a football while others are round like a baseball.

Our sun is one tiny speck in space. Space and all the stars in it go on for trillions and trillions of miles. Even the nearest star to the earth, the sun, is so far away a spaceship could not get to it in one person's lifetime.

Stars are evidence that objects in space are very, very old. We are just beginning to learn about all the secrets that stars hold. Someday, by studying the stars, scientists may begin to unlock these secrets of outer space.

Think Critically

1. What is the name of the galaxy that the earth and our sun are in? What kind of galaxy is it?

2. What will happen to the sun billions of years from now?

3. What is one way to tell stars apart?

4. How is the sun the same as other stars?

5. What did you learn about the sun that surprised you? Explain.

 Science

Look It Up Look up information about galaxies in an encyclopedia or on the Internet. Then write down some facts that interest you.

School-Home Connection With a family member, look at the stars in the sky. Draw a picture of what the stars look like to you.